Fleeting Moments

POEMS AND SONGS

MICKEY AND ZACHARY TAMER

Email: ztamer13@gmail.com
Website: zacharytamer.com

ISBN 10: 0-9974031-0-1
ISBN 13: 978-0-9974031-0-7

Cover Photo by Zachary Tamer

For our wives:

The reason we write poetry, drink whiskey,

and have short life expectancies.

This book is a collaboration of poems written by my father, Mickey Tamer (MT), and me (ZT). Our poems may touch on the similar topics of life, death, finding and losing religion, and love. These emotional themes come from our own vantage points and reflect our different ages, experiences, and writing styles, while still sharing many similarities. After all, we are our own scientific experiments of nature and nurture.

Contents

Worke

The leaves in the Garden
Were perpetually green
A few drops of water
For just the right sheen

Little need for thinking
Much less for speech
Always low hanging fruit
Within easy reach

No need for work
Nor for luck
The life of a king?
Or the life of a duck?

Like a rich man's children
Often bearing the scorn
Of becoming no more
Than the day they were born

So we traded the garden
For a working man's plight
And give thanks to Eve
For taking the first bite

Filament

A flicker of light in a cellar
Desperately clings to shadows,
Casting antique yellow incandescence.
A cobweb, a pull cord, a paint can,
A trunk, photos and toys
Flashing in and out of existence.
Darkness awaits its invitation.
Listless currents of heat
Losing ground
Wire and thread
Barely hanging on
finding a melting point.
With the slightest pop
the room disappears
leaving nothing more
than forgotten memories
of a time that used to shine.

Twilight

Now shadows are soft
And colors are muted
Now all is quiet
Solemnly still
Now just a breath
Between day and night
When love, hate, even time
Stand down
Hush!
It's twilight time

Oh Boy

I'm January
On an island retreat
A Texas boy
With shoes on both feet
I'm a drunkard
Sitting at the bar
A teen
With my first car
I couldn't stop smiling
If you knocked
Out my teeth
I'm gonna feel good
Till they hang a wreath
I'll have no more time
For sadness and grief
I thank you both for
Making me insane
It's your creation
And Olive is her name

Fleeting Moments

Never before has a fleeting moment seemed to last so long
She passed wearing a smile that reminded me of a song.
The bar was packed but she moved through crowds with grace
Oh the hippy girl with curls and an olive face.

Put back the tonic, and shot down the gin
Cast my eyes and there she was again.
Dancing lazily to the rhythms of the band
The lyrics to the music I would later understand.

These fleeting moments these passing faces
Oh these abandoned houses and forgotten places.
Sun drenched memories of a shadow in the light
Moon washed Raven silhouettes on a snowy night.

Oh this river floods my sleepless dreams
where everything's as cryptic as it seems.
Oh just to see her olive face once more
To do things differently than I did before
To at least say hello before she walks out the door.

Burial Grounds

Dust flies into the face of a young man with red dirt on his clothes.
The lines on his face tell me that he is nearly fifty years old
the lines lie and give him twenty extra years he has not yet seen.
Calloused hands grip a splintered shovel and dig the clay from the
unforgiving ground.
Dried blood streaks his fingers like the numerous sunsets he has
seen streak the sky.
Death smiles at him every day,
And all he can do is smile back and laugh.
He knows that one day
Someone else will hear the hollow sound
Of dirt hitting his wooden chest.

In the Last Hours of the Day

In the last hours of the day
We shouldn't waste time on small talk
We should only speak of tender times
Or better yet not speak at all
And only share the moment
In the last hours of the day

I can't know if we will walk again hand in hand
When dusk and night meet
But I know you will remember always
The time we shared
And the love we made

The times we tried and won and tried and failed
Are less than trivial
All that matters is the glow in your eyes
And the warmth of your heart
As we stand together
Sharing what must be pure love
In the last hours of the day

Autumn

The weeds have taken over
Vines are climbing too
Crept in while I was napping
Like the morning dew

My gardens have sent winners
To the county fair
But lately vines
Control the lion's share

A bluebird carried seeds
From my flagging spot
A nascent farmer
Starting her own plot

A twilight voice says
In his whispering way
"There must be night
Before a new day"

The weeds have taken over
As weeds always will
Like Kudzu covering
An old grist mill

Smashing Pumpkins in the Sky

"You can never ever leave
without leaving a piece of youth."
-Billy Corgan

We all sat cross legged on the bedroom floor
Talking about Smashing Pumpkins.
A group of young ruddy faced cousins
arguing about lyrics and their meanings.
My mind was all guitars and drums
The words were all just secondary.
But you seemed to understand
The reason behind each rhyme
The emotions inside each lyric.
While time ticked on
calendar pages kept turning
You perfected your crafts
Always sketching and singing.
Reticent to share your talents
I used to think you were embarrassed
Now I have a better understanding.
Though you may be leaving
Your art show will soon begin.
Your new audience is the globe.
No limit to your scale or scope.
Your canvas the atmosphere
Your voice will travel on the wind

In every setting sun
You are the orange glow
smashing pumpkins in the sky.
The northern lights
The harvest moon
A star speckled pasture
The winter's first snow.
A signature hidden
In the passing clouds above.
Each day a new masterpiece
Each breeze a concerto
Each brush stroke a reminder
You are everywhere we know.

The Rose

When the rose was picked
It left only thorns behind
But when I close my eyes
I see it clear in my mind
Pure white with dew drops
Hanging like tears
An image
I will cherish
For years
A picture embossed
On a page
Never to Blemish
Or tarnish with age

The Nightingale

The nightingale's song changed
Red to yellow, green and blue
Gave a soft glow to my heart
And put a light step
In my shoe
This little bird has flown
But has left behind
Ascending pure notes
Forever soft on my mind

Whiskey in my Coffee

When I woke this morning
I didn't feel like myself.
There was a tear on my pillow
That was still salty and wet.
Though I don't recall hearing
My wife must have cried
I know one thing for sure
Those tears weren't mine.
I take my coffee black
And my whiskey neat.
I eat my steak rare
And my voice booms when I speak.
Inhaling the robust vapor
Steeping at the top of my mug
I sat contemplating
My day through the dawn.
My thoughts soon rambled
Following my eyes to the trees.
I was thinking of Carolina
and all the miles between.
Morning dew must have fallen
Something splashed in my cup.
My face sticky with moisture
must be the steam wafting up.
Today my coffee seems so bitter

Adding some whiskey couldn't hurt.

With a flick of the wrist

I light a cigar

Blue plumes of smoke burn my eyes.

Another tear drop has fallen

I tell myself more lies.

I feel a hand on my shoulder

And a voice in my ear

Drink your coffee black

And your whiskey straight

eat your steak rare

and stay out too late

but when the day is done

Wear your tears plain on your face.

Going Home

Now there is no need
For approving smiles
Or sympathizing blues
No judicial wink
To let me know
If I'm out or if I'm in
There is no need
To walk miles
In someone else's shoes
Or let my shoulders sink
If I score low
On a scale from 1 to 10

I leave behind parties crowded
With forced grins
And plates with heavy garnish
But just a spot of meat.
I leave behind packed rooms
Where I am alone.
I leave behind parties shrouded
With false friends
Searching for that tarnish
To make their night complete
I leave you to your gloom
I'm going home

Home

We warm by the fire
In our most casual clothes
You sleep in the rocker
Reading glasses
On the tip of your nose
I move the blanket
To cover your feet
I think we must be home

You wake so gently
That you hardly stir
Your eyes seeing
Little more
Than a blur
Your lips curve softly
In a misty smile
I think we must be home

The coals of the fire
Are golden and red
You set your book on the table
Take your glasses from your head
I grin as you mumble
Something about sleep
I know we must be home

Requiem for Mickey's Place

It's just a building
No one was hurt
Just bricks from clay
Laid over concrete on dirt

But if you have the time,
If it's not too much trouble
Could you stop by
And sift through the rubble

There are a few things
I'd like to retrieve
A few friendly spirits
Before they leave

Spirits of those passed on
And of those still here
All there in the ashes
I see them so clear

The first on my list
Is strong as an ox
But gentle and kind
And smart as a fox

I've seen him shake a tree
Sixty feet high
While pecans fell
Like hail from the sky

You'll find him soon
Oh, anyone could
When he starts laughing
Like a devil gone good

The reason for
This gleeful rage
Would be sitting on a pop crate
Looking pensive and sage

There he would sit
Poised for the strike
Waiting for an argument
If it takes him all night

For my part
A good example he'd set
For he never gave up
And I'm sure he hasn't yet

Standing beside him
With a Fresca in hand
Was a very fine lawyer
But a much better man

Oh there's one
You must find
To us kids
He was
Generous and kind

Taught me stick shift
In a Chevy Belle Air
If I ruined the car
He wouldn't care

Love for us kids
Was simply a fact
He loved us
And we loved him back

But wait!
Don't go
Only now I discovered
What I should already know

Looking in my mirror
The reflection I see
Is my friends
Looking back at me

But the faces
I see the most
Are the store's owners
Or should I say hosts

Cigar

A tightly rolled Phillies blunt
Is held at attention
Between his teeth.
Smoke slowly tumbles
From his nose and mouth,
Its sweet rustic odor.

Every day the cigar burnt further down
But dwindled in such small amounts
That no one noticed.
It seemed that it would cheat death;
With each puff it looked no closer to the end.
A magician
With the unlikely act of never disappearing.

Day by day, month by month and year by year
It slowly wore down
Until finally,
The man with squirrel tails for eyebrows
And a mustache stolen from Graucho Marx
Was no longer allowed to smoke.

No inhalation
He just let the ember smolder
While chewing on the end

The magician's trick, it seemed
Had begun to fizzle.
While all eyes were on Houdini
In utter disbelief.

The cigar now began to deteriorate rapidly.
Its old brown, tightly rolled paper
Started to unravel,
Leaving only the crumbling innards,
And one end deformed and amputated
From the incessant chewing.
Until all that was left
Were the ashes of a trick
That never could have lasted,
And the smell of the cigar that still lay there burning.

Mingling Thoughts in the Laundromat

The walls are a dingy yellow,
Covered in grime and splattered mud.
The floors are the usual speckled tile
With pieces of gum
Smashed on the ground for so long
They have turned a dark grey
And become a part of the décor.
A snack machine and two arcade games
Sit pleadingly in the corner
For you to give them what money you have left.
12 dryers spin the colors
Of every one's life in plain sight.
While two of the doors swing idly open
Inhaling the dust and smells
Of this contradictory place.

It costs only $1.25
To wash your memories away
And 25cents to burn away the past
For fifteen blissful minutes.
It takes most many more quarters
To make their everyday toils scream from the heat.
When it's all over
Everyone has a new life in a basket
But this place still reeks of their sorrow.

Carousel

I saw the clown with the evil grin
And the horse with the frightened eye
Saw her smile and jumped right in
Knowing I should pass on by
The big cats bobbed around
Excited by the chase
Just ahead the zebra frowned
Wary of their cold embrace
She slid from the Panthers back
With smooth feline ease
Moving in to attack
As softly as a breeze
Her eyes, cold and blue,
Stopped my breath and froze my feet
I felt her purr and coo
Too late to retreat
Opening my callow eyes wide
I finally saw my plight
Trapped on this ride
Too weak to flee or fight
With ease I could see
The story of my fate
My heart was soon to be
Sliced upon her plate
But the excitement of the game

Was now a gaping yawn
She grabbed the lion's mane
Then quickly she was gone
In shame I crawled away
From that nightmare ride
I had been such easy prey
Stumbling on desire and pride
If ever I pass by again
Closer than a mile
Looking for a mate or friend
I'll search deeper than a smile

A Tree for all Seasons

Winter

Virulent winter gusts bluster through rickety bones.
Rattling limbs reach towards the sky and exalt the effort.
The wind recoils at the taunt and strikes with more force.
Bending and arching toward the ground
The branches fight back against the gale
Bough smacking against bough
The pressure begins to mount.
Appendages hit the earth.
The squall gives a slight reprieve.
A hush comes over the forest.
The trees will have some rest
Swathed in the last snows of winter.

Spring

New babies are born
I'll put on some girth
Life flows again
From sweet Mother Earth
I dine once more
On autumn's sweet decay
Sleep at night
And drink rain or sun

Each day
I'm part of life's matrix
That never rests
Always an inn
Always a guest

Summer

Lightning crackles in the distance
Threatening fire in the woods
Thunder vibrates to my heartwood
Rousting transients from their slumber.
The violence of a summer storm
A welcome repose from the heat.
Tomorrow the sun will rise again
Scorching my sodden bark.
Leaving a beautiful chestnut tinge.
My leaves smile towards the sun
Thankful for the light
Drowsy from the heat.
These lazy summer days
Have made me grow weary.
My ancient limbs droop in the blazing sun
Casting shadows where children run and play.
Sheltered from the oppressive rays
They stumble on the roots of my beginning
While they climb nearer to my new beginnings end.
These old bones take pleasure

In saccharine summer dreams
Of an autumn breeze yet to come.

Autumn

My acorns are falling
In clusters on the ground
My leaves will soon follow
Dried to a pastel brown
Creating a seasoned buffet
Building dark humus
On top of red clay
By following
Nature's s scheme
I'll be nourished when awakened
From winter's dream
We all grow together
The small and the great
At times eating
Then filling the plate
Taking only
What I need
I never indulge
Gluttony or greed
Crisp air on my skin
An Autumnal treat
That relaxes my limbs
And lulls me to sleep

If only two legged

Creatures could see

The wisdom of what is

And not what they wish it to be

Under the Blazing Sun

Under the blazing sun
We're all sewn together as one
A mend on a sleeve
A new kind of weave
The spinning wheel continues to run

I wonder where I've been
Maybe a snake's new skin
A leaf on a tree
A cricket's knee
Or a mole on a chin

All go around the loop
Even before primeval soup
Boiled in a stew
Dropped in the loo
Parts of all kinds of goop

But I sit, sipping my tea
Wondering what I will be
I'm hoping that day
Is far far away
For now it's great being me

Nightfall

Glassy-eyed wolves
Gnaw on pumpkin rinds
While candle wax drips
Down doorsteps.
Jack-o'-lantern faces
Flicker in the distance
Casting menacing shadows
Of teeth popping seeds.
A moon sliver hangs
Filtered by passing clouds
Illuminating faces
Matted with orange guts.
Cursed by the carver
Damned on the doorstep
Extinguished come morning.

Take a Hike

Find your daydream down by the creek.

Act like a child, skip some rocks and skin your knees.

Wet logs and crisp brown leaves line your path.

Take a deep breath

Inhale your surroundings

Decay has never smelled so alive.

Underneath the forest's canopy, life is humming.

Birds sing solos while water trickles the rhythm.

Branches sway with the beat, true music in motion.

Underneath your feet, worms eat the earth

Tilling the soil for seeds that travel on wind and wing.

Watch your step but keep your eyes alert

Claw prints, paw prints, hooves and shoes

A mud stamped passport lets you know

you are not the only traveler on this road.

The rocks always remain silent

Protecting the secrets they hide.

The oldest stories at the top

Were once the beginning of the climb.

Cling to that slab of history.

Sky above you and trees below

A magnificent church with a view.

Take a hike, and let your senses go.

Fishing

I'm a little lazy
And move kind of slow
Fishin is about
The most fun I know
My line is in the water
I'm leaning on a tree
And wondering who
I'll have for company

I see a blue heron
Still as a stone
A handsome bird
But always alone.
If he found a mate
She couldn't stay
The way he sings
Would chase a mountain away

A streak of blue
With a certain flair
A kingfisher
Sails through the air
A trapeze artist
Whose soul was set free

His flight seems to say
"It's good to be me!"

I'm not the only lazy one
It would seem
Not ten feet away
A box turtle is lost in a dream
This day is so perfect
Who can tell
He might feel too good
To hide in his shell

Mama duck is fussing
With her ducklings in a row
Whatever she is teaching
They need to know
It's quite a sight
These mallards on parade
I look at nothing else
Until they fade

Yes I love fishin
But I better go
The moon is on the rise
And the sun is sinking low
I hate to leave

But it's late

Maybe next time

I'll bring a hook

And some bait

Hibernation

Huddled together
Like pack animals
Emanating heat.
While the snow
Dips and twirls
Its bitter dance
A warm blue light
Flickers from the den.
Darkness comes early
Bringing them together.
Limbs intertwined
Until spring
awakens
the night.

Work Revisited

All serenity is lost
The alarm screams
I stare into nothing
And try to remain in my dreams

I'm floating in Limbo
While the alarm is saying
"Get up you bum,
No time for playing."

My fist "kills" the clock
My feet hit the floor
One more day
Just one more

Chase a dollar
To fill my gut
To pay bills
What a rut

Thanks so much, Eve
For taking that bite
For your vain nature
And greedy appetite

All Flats

When you got no shine
You got no soul
And there's no reason to sing
When there's no feeling in notes.

When all the keys sound flat
but the piano's just been tuned
there's no reason to play
if the problem is you.

When all the strings are tight
But play like yarn
The days are much too long
And you can't sleep the night.

Maybe it's not the music
But the maker.
Maybe it's not the dance
But the shaker.

Love in the Hills

Things don't seem as bad as they used to
No nothing hurts as bad anymore
The fields are green with grass
the sun is shining down on you.

Pale legs curled between a shadow
Your silhouette penciled in the hills
Leaves never turn brown
They live on in Technicolor

No things don't seem as bad as they used to
I let go of the pain
The winds are always changing
But you… you remain the same

Smile and light the night sky
Thirty two brilliant stars
paint art in the atmosphere
and spotlight the pasture side.

Oh things are so much better now
The dandelions turn to wine
And the buttercups stay gold
Hand in hand
We sprawl in the sun

Motionless jumping jacks
Cookie cutters to the sky
Etched into constellations
Even after we die.

The Dance

The room was alive
With a West African beat
A swirling display
Of heads hips and feet
Showing colors
Alive and bright
A dazzling
Mating rite

Spring jonquils gave way
To summertime heat
The dance now moved
With a syncopated beat
Dancers paired with
Their heart's mate
Came to unwind
Or to celebrate
The melodies and motion
Had a different tune
More from the earth
Less from the moon

Hot Julys became
Pleasant Septembers
Once roaring fires

Now glowing embers
The music morphed
A full orchestral sound
Jeans and short skirts
Are long tails and gowns
Strauss sets the pace
For dancers to move
With a certain easy grace

As change marks time
On the clock
The dance is the tick
And the tock
Moving to tunes we choose
From the waltz
To Blue Suede Shoes
Until
Our music stops

The Big C

We are a generation of cancers
Our fathers,
Our mothers,
Our wives,
Our friends,
Their brothers,
Their mothers,
We are them.
We are born.
We mourn.
We curse the sky.

I am the sun
your dinner,
your water,
your air.
I am the reason
They say
That life isn't fair.
Breathe me in.
Breath me out.
I am your everything.
I am your everywhere.
Your life.
Your love.
Your final despair.

Thank you

I had reached
The blood red horizon
Where the great thief
Takes all you have
And casts you out to sea

His hands were in my pockets
As my boat was docking
Then you came
And pulled me free

Now the dreams
He was stealing
Are here when I wake
And the boat
Has drifted from shore

You have brought
Hope and salvation
And the blood red horizon
Is distant once more

More Than I See

She blew
I blew it
Now it's all blown.
Not much of a surprise.
Put on a hat
Try and hide.
No one knows,
No one knows,
Who you are,
What you became,
When it all came to an end.
Grow a beard,
Cover your face.
No one knows,
No; no one knows
That your life
Is such a disgrace.
My arms are tired
From climbing towards the top.
Maybe I'll just stop;
Find something,
Something more comfortable,
Something in the middle,
Just try to blend in
Maybe make a friend.

Find a girl
With a hand to lend
Help me find the top
Then I can stop
Oh; I can stop
Stop running
Stop falling
Stop hiding
I just want to be
To be
More than I see.

Slumped

Sliding down a hill of rocks
When you're already on your knees
Doesn't make you bleed
It makes you seethe.
I need a change of scenery
I need to change my speed.
I've been running on empty
And giving up on my dreams.
I've left before
Tried to close the door
On what I'm not sure.
Sometimes it's me
Sometimes it's you
Sometimes the world
My point of view.

I'm tired
Of closing doors
Wearing band aids,
I need to take off the hinges
Start rebuilding bridges
Turn off the lights
Open the blinds
Run the show
Make my life my own.

Rose of the Winds

When my ship is lost at sea
And I can no longer see dry land
I can count on you to redirect me
I know you will take me by the hand.

For years my atlas was torn and faded
Spinning in circles finding dead ends
In the deepest waters I had waded
When all I needed was my rose of the winds

Casting out into this vast ocean
Happy for even the smallest bite
After years I dropped that notion
Realizing there were better fish in sight

Diving to the darkest depths I searched
Hoping to come up with more than the bends
Many times I swayed and lurched
When all I needed was my rose of the winds

She was sitting in the corner, just to my right side
In a place where I'd been many times before
Her smile was the sun that changed my ebbing tide
Dropping anchor I would set sail no more.

I used to curse those years spent without you, wandering astray
The brackish air still burns but now I see how the horizon
extends.
If I had never traveled to points south I wouldn't be where I am
today
Facing towards true north with my sweet rose of the winds.

Bittersweet

No need to tend the fire
The wood has all been burned
The book seems unfinished
But the final page has turned
The crocus and the jonquil
Stand in defiance of the snow
Warmer suns are coming
As the embers lose their glow
The chill in the cabin
Goes deep into the soul
Outside spring unfolds
As cold grips the final coal
I loved the book
Though it didn't seem complete
I thought of spring and winter
And how they're bittersweet
Some book endings
I guess we'll never know
It's spring outside the cabin
Open the window let her go

Wedding Day

Standing at the altar
A lump rising in my throat
I watch you walk down the aisle
My hands search for something to do
My lips
Curl up in a smile

Love isn't much
Left alone in the dark
Where it wilts and dies
And I wasn't much
Until you came along
With love's light
In your eyes

Now you're beside me
As I recall my life
Before you came in
It was carnivals
Merry Go rounds
And games nobody wins

How could I have
So many friends
Always crowding my home

Yet lack
The special touch
That kept me
From being alone

Slipping a gold band
On your ring finger
I know our love
Won't end
I could be happy
The rest of my life
With you as my only friend

We'll never play
Carnival games
Where love is a game
Of pretend
We'll never be alone
In a room full of friends

Now we pledge forever
We'll be together
Whatever may come
Through joy and sorrow
We'll face tomorrow
As one

No my love wasn't much
Until it bathed in your sunshine
And started to grow
Whatever we do
It will be me and you
Until our hair
Is whiter than snow

The Carpenter

A whirling saw blade
flings particles skyward.
Sawdust hangs in a sunbeam;
in that moment time floats.
Serrated blades of green grass
stand tall and menacing
but soon are blanketed
under a soft layer of dust.

II
Cherry, Walnut,
Maple, Oak,
Mahogany, Hickory
Poplar and Pine
hues of the earth
cover the workshop floor.
From this clutter
timber is measured
cut, planed
dovetailed, sanded
shaped and primed.
They become
your cabinets
your trim
your floors;

the bones of a house.
They are tables
filled with coffee
clattering plates
board games and food.
Soaking up secrets
laughter and tears.
Witness to breakups
first kisses, weddings
funerals and births.
The creaking of boards
The wind in the rafters
Front porch swings
And mended fences.
Work done yesterday
or one hundred years before.
The spirit of the carpenter imbued
Into his craft and into our lives.

III

The carpenter's wife scans the room.
Her cabinets have no doors or drawers
The floors need to be sanded and stained
The walls need to be patched and painted
The tables and chairs are all off kilter.
She smiles, and exhales a sigh of relief.
At least I didn't marry a dentist.

IV

When I was a child
I despised that buzzing shrill.
Saw blades whining
The monotonous thud of hammers
Always waking me too early on Saturday mornings.
The sawdust that clung to the high grass
Only a nuisance that reminded me of waking from a dream.

V

Tonight the rich aroma of toasting wood
hung on the crisp fall air.
Eyes closed, head high, I inhaled deeply;
my body warmed and energized.
Memories came wrapped in moonlight:
The sun rarely woke the night's deep slumber
when we loaded tools into my father's truck.
We spoke early morning words
in hushed voices of the dawn,
The floor of the truck littered with pencil shavings,
The cab steeped with sweat and coffee grounds;
Infused with the sounds of Ray, Otis, and Allman Brothers.
We worked through the moments between dark.

VI

When he gave me my first tool belt
I puffed out my chest and put my shoulders back
buckling that canvas and leather pouch at my waist.
On the surface I was the Outlaw Josey Wales
Deeper down it meant one day I could be like my father.
I buckled that tool belt less
When I turned my tassel left.
I made my own path
with new twists and curves.
Along the way I have stumbled
And made wrong turns
but what I heard
between the clanging hammers
and the saw tooth's zipping bite
always leads me back
to the right path in my life.
I watched and I listened
And this is what I learned.
That love is the foundation
which a family builds upon.
A carpenter can build a house
But the bones don't make a home.
How to treat a woman.
How to tell a joke.
When to keep quiet.
And when to take a stand.
How to drink whisky

And how to throw a punch

When to make your own way

And when to take a helping hand.

Through all of these lessons,

The laughter and love,

I saw the man

I hope I can someday become.

The Word

I can't seem to say it
Though it's a simple word
My lips quiver and
My eyes get blurred

Let me try again
It's not that hard to say
Just a moment
I have to turn away

To me it sounds
Like a broken gong
Or like a bad note
In the middle of a song

I hear it in the distance
Like thunder rolling down
My body shudders
From my head to the ground

I've got to say it
Though it makes me cry
The very word I've dreaded
Goodbye

The Cycle

He dreamt of being a leaf falling to the ground
One among many but still standing out.
To float silently on the breeze
A stirring energy that nobody sees.
Something that makes you move
And you don't know why
A force so strong
It can move the clouds in the sky.

We all want something that makes us feel
Anything; anything at all that lets us know it's real.
He shot a blackbird; sank to his knees and cried
The bird fell like a stone and the boy inside died.
Death frees you from questions
And frees questions you've never asked.
A force so strong
That all of the answers are masked.

He dreamt of being someone's dandelion seeds
Infecting the ground with happy yellow weeds.
To spread life with a breath
But still it brought death.
We all want a reason to live
Not a reason to die.
A force so strong
we can't stop it if we try.

Time

The hourglass sands
Are wet and stopped
 Sofia sits at her desk
And stares at the clock
The teacher's watch
won't slow down
His youth was stolen
With hardly a sound

A cantankerous child
This thing called time
Making hurry move slowly
And slow
Really unwind
We chase this
Frankenstein creation
Out of control
Till we find we've lost
Both body and soul

How can we know
When we're hungry or tired
When it's time
To grow up
Or time to expire

I think I'll
Throw everything away
That keeps time
So time can't
Keep me
Or keep me in line

My Brothers Keeper

Sifting through garbage
Behind the cafe
He wipes coffee grounds
From a discarded soufflé
His hands now shaky
Since losing his grip
Once flowing thoughts
Have become a slow drip
Whispered memories
And flecks of time
Give no bearing
To his drifting mind

Smelling of urine
And other body waste
He moved into the crowd
To his own private space
In a river of people
In a great rush
He goes untouched
Not a bump or a brush
We wash our hands
In Pontius Pilot's sink
But the stain in our hearts
Soon begins to stink

A mother once
Held him tight to her breast
He once passed love notes
To the girl in the next desk
Was he first in his class
With a proper cap and gown
Or did he tip his pallet just so
To fit the class clown?
Probably had a favorite song
And a hero or two
Now he fights rats
For the remnants of stew

An urban gypsy
With no name or face
One day will leave
With barely a trace
His sin remains,
A waste of time
His sickness
A troubled mind
We will give him a name
And a tag on his toe
Forever he will be
John Doe

I've Got a Clue

Should the earth
Thank Father Sun
For giving her light
Or should the sun
Be grateful
For such a beautiful sight
I don't know which
Answer is true
But I've got a clue
In you

Should fish
Thank the oceans
Where they swim free
Or should the waters
Be happy
For such lively company
I don't know which
Answer is true
But I've got a clue
In you

Should the roots
thank the leaves
or the rivers the rain

They're all
Tied together
In the same refrain
I know which
Answers are true
Because I've got a clue
In you

My Song To You

Do we sing a round robin song
Never knowing the meaning or tune?
Are we pulled into a black hole of nothing
Or guided to a warming light of love?
Is there a crossing over, a reuniting
Of those that went before us
Are we marching toward or away from something?
I know we will keep marching
Because we must.
I know I will always love you
For delivering me into this beautiful confusion.
I have been loved more than I deserve
And that's enough for me.
I have a song I sing every day
I know the words and what I mean to say.

Sharing

I tried to paint a feeling
One I had to share
I soon discovered
I didn't have the flair

I tried to sing a song
To open up my heart
But every note was like a goat
Then it fell apart

I tried a violin and bow
To make some music sweet
The folly of the first volley
Was my third defeat

My talents are so few
I finally must confess
Maybe words in verse
Won't be such a mess

The Wild Mongoose

Part 1

A hammock hangs between two walnut trees
Swaying listlessly in the summer heat.
Work weary ants march below
In the desiccated Virginia clay.
They make their way back home to the queen
With a feast of larvae, crumbs and leaves.
The stifling remnants of a breeze
Pass through the tree's branches.
Green walnut grenades fall with a thud
Scattering land mines around mother and son.
The boy's limbs hang carelessly from their fort
Questions float on the wings of birds in flight.

Part 2

Don't talk too loud or it might hear you.
A grin plays on the boy's face
A mix of fear and doubt.
Watch your feet! There it goes!
Knobby knees crash back into the hammock
The fort begins to sway.
You were lucky you got your feet in the fort so fast
The wild mongoose nearly got your little toe.
He creeps in the trees and rustles the roosting birds
They have been singing out trying to warn you

But you did not sit still and listen to their advice.

Now you know why the birds took flight.

The mongoose flung the hanging walnuts towards the earth

Using his razor sharp claws to clip them from their stems

Then he used his red tail to whip them towards us.

The wind protected us and swayed the hammock out of harm's way.

Now you know why the walnuts came showering down.

The ants have formed an army to protect the queen

Food is gathered so they can stay safe at home

when the wild mongoose goes on the attack.

I bet you didn't even see him when he snapped at your toes.

Like a flash of lighting or a humming bird's wings

He was by your feet and at the same moment back in the trees.

Oh look there he goes all the way to the top between the leaves.

I understand why you didn't see him

His colors change like a chameleon.

He was as orange as the clay on the ground

And as brown as the bark on the trees.

As green as the walnuts

And his tail as red as the setting sun.

I know it is hard to believe he hasn't caught us yet

You think I must be telling tales.

He hunts by sound and sight.

If we keep our voices to a whisper

And stay inside of our fort

The mongoose will never be able to find us.

If you close your eyes and stay very still

The mongoose will lose all hope and leave.

In an hour we may be able to make it back to the house.

Part 3

Today I let the red setting sun capture my shadow.

Legs sprawling off the side of my hammock,

A green walnut thuds like a golf ball

In the orange Virginia clay.

I pull my toes back inside my fort.

Close my eyes and smile.

Maybe in an hour

I can make it back home.